MW00898784

ELLEN OCHOA

By Joan Stoltman

Gareth Stevens
PUBLISHING

Please visit our website, www.garethstevens.com. For a free color catalog of all our high-quality books, call toll free 1-800-542-2595 or fax 1-877-542-2596.

Cataloging-in-Publication Data

Names: Stoltman, Joan.
Title: Ellen Ochoa / Joan Stoltman.
Description: New York : Gareth Stevens Publishing, 2019. | Series: Little biographies of big people | Includes glossary and index.
Identifiers: LCCN ISBN 9781538218426 (pbk.) | ISBN 9781538218402 (library bound) | ISBN 9781538218433 (6 pack)
Subjects: LCSH: Ochoa, Ellen–Juvenile literature. | Women astronauts–United States--Biography–Juvenile literature. | Astronauts–United States–Biography–Juvenile literature. | Women scientists–United States–Biography–Juvenile literature. | Hispanic American women–Biography–Juvenile literature.
Classification: LCC TL789.85.O25 S76 2019 | DDC 629.450092 B–dc23

Published in 2019 by
Gareth Stevens Publishing
111 East 14th Street, Suite 349
New York, NY 10003

Copyright © 2019 Gareth Stevens Publishing

Designer: Sarah Liddell
Editor: Kate Mikoley

Photo credits: series art Yulia Glam/Shutterstock.com; cover, p. 1 WJBscribe/ Wikimedia Commons; p. 5 Bardocz Peter/Shutterstock.com; p. 7 NASA/Handout/ Getty Images Sport/Getty Images; pp. 9, 15 NASA/Handout/Hulton Archive/ Getty Images; p. 11 Jasonanaggie/Wikimedia Commons; p. 13 Time Life Pictures/ Contributor/The LIFE PIcture Collection/Getty Images; pp. 17, 21 (main) Ras67/ Wikimedia Commons; p. 19 NASA/Handout/Getty Images News/Getty Images; p. 21 (inset) BotMultichillT/Wikimedia Commons.

Printed in the United States of America

CPSIA compliance information: Batch #CS18GS: For further information contact Gareth Stevens, New York, New York at 1-800-542-2595.

CONTENTS

Boldface words appear in the glossary.

Ellen's Childhood

Ellen Ochoa (oh-CHO-ah) was born in Los Angeles, California, in 1958. She was the middle child in a family of five children. Ellen and her family moved to a city near San Diego, California, when she was young.

NEVADA

UTAH

CALIFORNIA

● LOS ANGELES

SAN DIEGO ●

ARIZONA

MEXICO

PACIFIC
OCEAN

5

Ellen's grandparents on her father's side were from Mexico. Sadly, because of this, some people treated her father's family poorly when he was young. Ellen's father didn't want his own children treated badly, so Ellen and her **siblings** weren't taught Spanish.

ELLEN'S
SON, WILSON

When Ellen was still a baby, her mother started taking **college** classes. It took her 22 years to finish, but she showed Ellen how important **education** was. In high school, Ellen was the top student of her class.

"I believe a good education can take you anywhere on Earth and beyond."

—Ellen Ochoa

What to Be?

Ellen didn't know what to study in college. She'd played the **flute**, so she thought about studying music. She thought about writing news. She thought about studying **engineering**, but was told women couldn't be engineers. Finally, Ellen chose to study **physics**.

11

Then Everything Changed

After studying physics, Ellen followed her heart and went to school for engineering! While Ellen was working on her engineering degree, Sally Ride became the first American woman to go to space. Ellen realized she could become an **astronaut**, too!

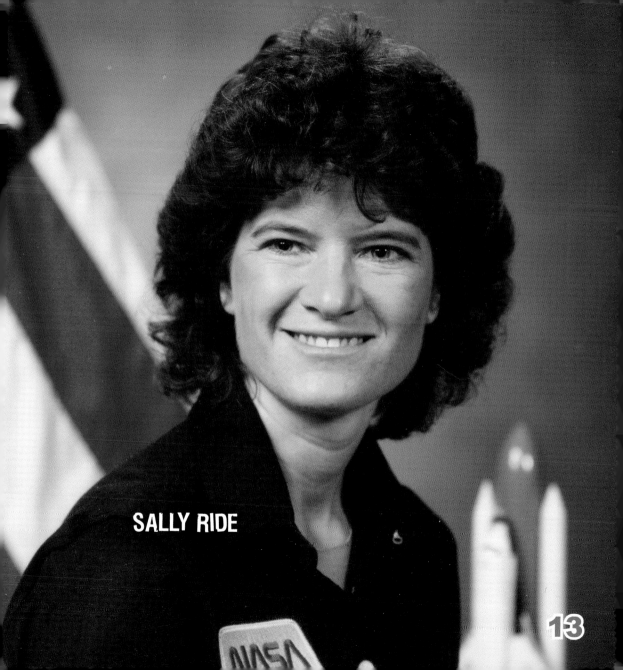

SALLY RIDE

13

Try, Try Again

Ellen wasn't picked the first two times she tried to become an astronaut. But this didn't stop her! She went to work for **NASA**, invented special science tools, and learned to fly aircraft. Five years after she first tried, Ellen was chosen to be an astronaut in 1990!

The First Hispanic Woman in Space!

Like all astronauts, Ellen spent time training and learning. She studied and practiced working with special robots. This would be one of her many jobs in space. Ellen went to space in 1993, 1994, 1999, and 2002. She was in space for around 1,000 hours total!

It wasn't easy spending time in space, but Ellen was doing very important work. In 1999, Ellen was part of the first team to dock at the International Space Station! While in space Ellen was able to talk to her family using special video tools!

19

Not Done Yet

Ellen still works for NASA today. Since 2013, she's been in charge of the Johnson Space Center in Houston, Texas. Schools across the country are named after her! She's a true example of how hard work can help you reach your dreams.

JOHNSON
SPACE CENTER

21

GLOSSARY

astronaut: someone who works or lives in space

college: a school after high school

education: the knowledge, skill, and understanding that you get from going to school

engineering: the use of science and math to build better objects

flute: a musical instrument that is shaped like a thin pipe and that is played by blowing across a hole near one end

NASA: the National Aeronautic and Space Administration, the government group that is in charge of studying and traveling to space

physics: a science that deals with matter and energy

sibling: a brother or sister

FOR MORE INFORMATION

BOOKS

Juarez, Christine. *Ellen Ochoa*. North Mankato, MN: Capstone Press, 2017.

McAneney, Caitie. *Women in Space*. New York, NY: PowerKids Press, 2016.

Schwartz, Heather E. *Astronaut Ellen Ochoa*. Minneapolis, MN: Lerner Publications, 2018.

WEBSITES

Makers Profile: Ellen Ochoa
www.makers.com/ellen-ochoa
Watch a video of Ellen Ochoa talking about her life and learn more about her on this page.

NASA Kids' Club
www.nasa.gov/kidsclub/index.html
Play games and learn more about NASA on this website.

INDEX